The Container

How do we know God's
presence is with us?

The Container

How do we know God's
presence is with us?

Matt Rawlins

A*muze*ment Publications
Salem, Oregon

Dedication

This book is dedicated to my son
Joshua. A gift from God.

The Container

Then Moses said to him, "If your Presence does not go with us, do not send us up from here. How will anyone know that you are pleased with me and with your people unless you go with us? What else will distinguish me and your people from all the other people on the face of the earth?"
Deu. 15-16

Chapter 1

The father sat next to the hospital bed
that held his son, "Can you hear me?
The doctor says you're going to make it.
Did you hear that? It's going to be okay.
If you need anything, squeeze my
hand."

The father held his son's hand in his and
loosened his tie with his other hand. The
night would not be nearly as long now
knowing he would have his son in the
morning.

Sleep finally overcame the father and
the next thing he realized his hand was
being gently squeezed. As soon as he
realized what was happening he looked
up and saw his son's eyes barely open.

"It's Okay son, don't speak. It was
pretty close there but the operation went

well and they were able to stop the bleeding. They will have the tube out of your nose tomorrow morning. Just rest."

The son closed his eyes and drifted back to sleep.

• • •

Later the next morning the father reentered the room after the doctor left and walked over to his son.

The son looked up and tried to grin, "I am really glad to have that thing out of my nose. It was like a bad dream."

"I must confess I'm glad to see you without those tubes. I could hardly stand the sight of all those things going in you."

The son looked around the room and then stated, "I have to say something quickly before I lose the courage."

The father nodded and sat down and the son took a long slow breath and said, "I realized last night when I was laying on the ground looking at my mangled car, not knowing whether I was going to live or die, that I was not walking with God." The son laid his head back and coughed. He lifted his head up and continued, "I have been half-hearted and more interested in money, cars and my position at work. I realized how cheap all those things were when weighed on the scales of life and death. I haven't listened to you for a while." The son leaned back again into the pillow and haltingly asked, "Can you tell me how to get my relationships right again?"

The father began to cry and whispered, "I would love to help. Let's spend time together over this next month and we can talk it all through. They say it will take that long for the breaks to set. I always loved a captive audience."

"Captive, yes," the son said looking at his leg in traction, "to this, but I think this is the first time I have not felt like a captive and I can listen."

"Get some rest. The doctor says you need to sleep and I will see you tonight. We can begin where ever you want."

"Cool," the son mumbled as he closed his eyes.

Chapter 2

The son began, "First of all, why does God put such a priority on relationships? I am not sure my relationship with my wife will make it. You saw how she looked at me."

The father nodded.

"Why do I have to need others? I just want to make it on my own."

"You never did like to admit you needed others. Remember when you sat in that tree all night because it was too dark for you to climb down but you refused to ask for help?"

"Yeah, I could hear you calling my name but I didn't want to admit I couldn't do it on my own. It was a long cold night."

"We sure were glad to see you the next morning," the father replied, "Now as to your question, I must say you have asked the most important question first. This may take awhile to understand. Let's start with your relationship with God. Let me tell you my understanding of the story of God creating us. You always liked a good story, so I will put it in a story form to keep you from falling asleep."

"Cool, go for it."

So the father began.

• • •

"We have to start at the beginning. God formed a shell of dust and then breathed into it the breath of life…

Adam awoke, complete in himself and yet incomplete alone. He was too young to know it, yet very quickly, know it he did. In a perfect world, learning was quick and painless. To admit a need was not a struggle, but a joy.

"God," Adam called out.

"Yes," God responded.

"I am confused. Words cannot explain my struggle but I will try. I have you, and you are enough. Yet, I cannot hold you within me. This makes me feel awkward. Did you make me this way?" Adam asked.

"Yes, I did."

"Why?"

"I have made you to be an expression of myself."

"You feel this way?" Adam asked puzzled.

God laughed out loud and said, "I AM Content."

"Then why?" Adam pressed.

"I wanted you to taste your incompleteness. I AM enough for you, and I WILL

BE flowing through you. Alone you will never be able to contain me. I have made you to be like a stream bed, in that, the flow of My Presence in you, like water, must be an ongoing process. My Presence will flow in and through you and this will keep you constantly dependent upon me as the source."

"I love your flowing through me. And yet I feel I want more. I long to hold your presence in a way that I cannot. Must I live with this incompleteness?" Adam asked.

"No, I only wanted you to taste your incompleteness so that you would welcome another aspect of who I am in your midst."

"Yes!" Adam raised his hands in sheer pleasure. "I am ready to see more of you."

"Then sleep my son and I will soon show you," the Lord whispered as Adam lay down and rested on the grass.

The CREATOR gently took a rib from Adam and formed a partner for him. A perfect fit.

Adam awoke and sat in anticipation.

God brought her forth to him.

Adam quickly jumped to his feet and stared.

She stared back.

"She is beautiful, Father," Adam exclaimed.

God saw their wonder and responded, "Share all that is in your heart with each other and there, I will dwell."

Adam and Eve gave themselves to each other in words and actions and their relationship was established. In this relationship God found a place for His Presence and it was the fullest expression of Himself that could be known on earth.

"In this way you will represent Us. We have created you. We are Three in One. Complete alone and yet only God as One. When you are alone We will flow through you individually, but as you share with each other, Our Presence will be contained in your relationship. You will model us in a small and yet splendid way. Complete in yourself and yet incomplete alone. The ongoing mystery of love."

• • •

The son held up his hand, yawned and asked, "What do you mean complete in himself and yet incomplete alone. You always told me God wanted to dwell in my heart. I am not sure I get it."

"I can see you are getting sleepy and reached your limit. I want you to think of a straw or a stream and think about their ability to contain water. We will talk more in the morning."

The son responded, "I have to do some of the work huh? I guess I'm in no hurry." He laid his head back and closed his eyes. He was soon asleep.

The father sat for a while with him and enjoyed just sitting next to his son. Finally he got up, kissed him on his forehead and whispered, "Good night. I will see you in the morning."

Chapter 3

The next morning the son began, "You know it's amazing how much time you have to think in this place. The nurses come in all night and wake you up just to see if you're all right. It is enough to drive you crazy."

"Use the quietness to catch up on some thinking you haven't done in a while. I have a sense God might be in it," the father said as he winked.

"I have more time than I know what to do with. You mentioned last night about a straw or a stream. I got distracted with a tube instead of a straw but I think it is the same thing."

"Good, tell me what you thought about?"

"A stream does contain or hold the water but only in the sense that it has more water coming into it to replace that which is going out. If the water were to stop entering it or moving through it then it could not contain water. It is the same with a tube or straw. It is not made to hold water or medicine but to allow it to pass through it."

"So why do you think God made us that way?" the father asked.

"I think I am only beginning to under-stand. He wanted to have a relationship with us so he made us like a straw or stream in that we could walk with him only as he flowed through us. That flowing would create a dependence on him. By why is he so hung up on our dependence on him?"

"I think the better question is why you and I are so hung up on our indepen-dence *from* Him? Let me continue with the story of Adam and Eve and see if it makes sense in exploring how we ended up where we are."

• • •

Time passed and Adam and Eve explored their new-found relationship. Physical pleasure was a part of it, but their fullest joy was in their ongoing discovery of each other in the words they used and how it expressed the things they learned.

One day Adam was on a walk by himself. He stopped by a flowing spring and listened to the water bubbling over the rocks. As he listened to the sounds, as if for the first time, he thought of Eve and how those sounds were like her laughter. She was a bubbling stream when she laughed. He quickly turned to find her to share this new idea with her. He could not wait to express in new words what she was like to him. Eve also brought her revelation of what Adam meant to her.

With each passing day they rejoiced in their individual uniqueness. This completeness of God flowing through them gave them new discoveries to share with each other. Their incompleteness in being alone was now a greater joy as they learned to bring these new discoveries to each other and by sharing them, build a relationship that provided a dwelling place for God's Presence in their midst. As their relationship grew so their capacity to accommodate more of God's Presence grew.

• • •

The devil also was pleased in their incompleteness and had plans of his own. He saw this open door and how God made Himself vulnerable to attack by making them incomplete alone. He took his chance to show them a new life. His life.

"Eve," the devil slurred.

"Yes," she replied.

"I have watched the beauty of your relationship with Adam."

"It is growing deeper and richer everyday," Eve stated in joy.

"Do you think it will last forever?"

"Oh, yes. It must."

"What about your relationship with God?"

"Oh, yes. We have all eternity to spend together."

"I wonder, has God put conditions on his love? I mean, did He say you will live with Him forever no matter what?"

"No," Eve said, "We will die if we eat from this one tree."

"So God has put conditions on you?" the devil questioned full of himself.

"Yes, we shall die if we eat of the tree," Eve responded.

"You surely won't die for you were made to contain the Almighty. How can that which was made to contain the Almighty die? He is eternal and His power is unending. In order for you to contain Him, you must be made of the same stuff. If you are made of the same stuff, you must be God."

Eve didn't hesitate, "We are only containers, I don't know how, but holding Him is different than being Him."

The devil walked away and said, "Are you sure? We will talk more later. Think about what I have said."

•　•　•

At a later time the devil found Eve and whispered to her again, "That which can contain God must be God. If you can hold God within you, surely then you must be able to be as He is."
Eve listened.

The devil continued, "He wants you to believe that you are 'only' a container.

Yet, He Himself implied that He is a container."

Eve nodded in agreement, "Yes, He suggested He is a container, three in one, and we are made in His image."

The devil pushed harder, "If He is a container, and you are a container, you are like Him. If then you take of this fruit, your eyes will be opened and the power you felt when He dwelt with you and Adam, you can now feel on your own, apart from Him."

Eve tasted the fruit and gave it to Adam who was with her and their eyes were opened.

• • •

"Adam, what have we done?" Eve asked after they had both eaten of the fruit.

Adam looked at the world around him with new eyes. "Before we were naked and yet clothed by our innocence. Now we are clothed," Adam pointed at the leaves, "and yet naked by our awareness."

Eve wept and looked at her mate, "I'm afraid. We now see as God can and this sight has cost us the very thing we sought to find."

Adam nodded in agreement, "I feel as if I'm exposed, vulnerable."

"Yes," Eve interrupted, "It's as if the very way I define myself has changed."

Adam walked over to a pool of water nearby and said, "Before, we were like this stream bed with pure water, clear and transparent flowing through us. The water's transparency revealed deeper beauty like the fish and different rocks and plants and then the water added beauty to it all by its movement reflecting the light." He reached into the pool of water and swirled it around so that it became cloudy and dirty. "Now the dirt from the stream bed has been stirred and the water is dirty. We block the beauty seen through us and have a bad taste. I find myself terrified the stream will run dry."

The earth trembled lightly. Adam and Eve froze. They looked at each other and knew He was coming. It was the sound of His steps as He walked in the garden. He was coming to be with them. That which had brought them the greatest pleasure before now filled them with terror. They would be seen, noticed, exposed before Him.

• • •

The father leaned back in the chair, looked at his son and said, "God asked for clarity as to what happened and then sends Adam and Eve out of the garden to protect them from eating of the Tree of Life and thus, living forever in this fallen state. Adam and Eve discover themselves in a new world. They find themselves in a world that is cursed and under new management. Anything they attempt to do now must be done by hard work and through painful labor.

Any container built from their relationship will now be flawed and distort the
pure water given."

• • •

"I hadn't thought of it that way," the son
replied.

"There is a lot of pain in our world
because of relationships and so we don't
want to get hurt. The answer is not
independence from everyone but dependence on the right person. He made
us so that our dependence on Him
would be a constant joy. We are the ones
who made it a pain by our selfishness."

The son reflected on the story and then
said, "God is infinite and that means
there is no limit to the amount of Him
that can flow through us. He made us
eternal so it can go on forever. That is a
completely new thought. All I have ever
thought about was an eternal church
service and that thought bored me to
death."

"You are catching on quickly. All He ever asked for was thanksgiving and respect as our response to Him. He simply wants a relationship with us and for us to relate to each other."

The son yawned and asked, "But you said earlier I am incomplete alone. What do you mean? If He dwells in me isn't that enough?"

"When you think that God dwells in you, if you think of it like a man dwelling in a house, the temptation is to think you can do it on your own with Him in you. But I think that is wrong way of looking at it. He is Three in One. In order for us to truly represent Him it cannot be done outside of a relationship with others. That is why He flows through you but dwells in your relationships. Without relationships you cannot fully represent God."

The son rested his head on the pillow and closed his eyes, "So many new ideas. I think that will get me through the day."

The father rose and stated, "Good, I will see you tomorrow."

Chapter 4

The son began, "Yesterday was interesting and my mind seemed full of thoughts. I know that we are made in His image. He is Three in One. I must confess a mystery to me. If what you're saying is true, and I accept it, then it seems that He made us so that only as we meet together can we hold or create a place where He will dwell."

The father nodded and said, "You know the scriptures that say,

"'For where two or three come together in my name, there am I with them.'" [1]

"'By this all men will know that you are my disciples, if you love one another.' [2]

"Or how about 'No one has beheld God at any time; if we love one another, God abides in us, and His love is perfected in us.' 3

"I will give you one last scripture, a prayer of Jesus, 'I in them and you in me. May they be brought to complete unity to let the world know that you sent me and have loved them even as you have loved me.'4 Our message is ultimately about relationships. Where we join together His Presence dwells. You know the story about Moses and the golden calf."5

• • •

The Israelites were a people who cared more about power than God's Presence. Moses had gone up the mountain and they thought he was dead so they asked Aaron to make a god for them. The didn't care who it was, just as long as they had power from a god. You can almost hear them call out to Aaron, "Make for us a god that will dwell with us and give us power to get us out of this place. After all, we are a container made by God, we must fill it with some power."

Aaron thought quietly and then spoke, "Bring me the gold you have."

The people brought the gold to Aaron and he fashioned a calf with the gold and then proclaimed, "For all you care, this is your god who brought you up out of Egypt."

The people rose the next morning and had a party and they all got drunk as they felt empowered to continue on in their journey. A god was once again with them.

• • •

The father sat back and continued on, "God listened to the people's arrogance. He was so angry at them that He was going to destroy them and start over again with Moses. His discussion with Moses sounded something like this…"

• • •

"Moses, they are a proud and obstinate people who don't care whose presence is among them. They only care that they get what they want as a result of power," the Lord shared painfully.

Moses replied, "They don't care if it is demonic or You who dwells among them. All they want is power. I am sorry they think so little of You, themselves and their relationships with each other."

"Leave me, that I may destroy them; and I will fulfill my plans for a great nation through you."

Moses entreated the Lord and said, "What will the nations think about You and Your Presence among the people? Will they think that You are not good or that You are not strong enough to do this? Think of the people that have gone before Israel and Your work to prepare them for Your Presence. You are the only True Presence, God. They are a special container."

So the Lord changed his mind and told Moses, "I have heard your intercession and will send an angel to go before you."

Moses entreated the Lord further, "Lord, what is it that separates us from all the other people in the land? That we are a container? No, any group can form a container. It is The Presence in the container that makes the container valuable. It is Your identity in us that holds us all together and gives us life. If Your Presence does not fill us, then do not lead us up from here. For how else can it be known that we have found favor in Your sight, unless Your Presence is with us and You go with us. Your filling the structure created by our relationships is the only thing that distinguishes us from all other people."

The Lord responded to this entreaty, "I will do what you have asked, for you have found favor in My sight and I know you by name."

• • •

"I think if God asked me I would have taken Him up on His offer to build a new nation through me," the son pondered out loud.

The father smiled, "I would have accepted His offer to have an angel go before me. They are powerful beings. But Moses understood that one thing and one thing alone separated the people and their relationships from all other peoples on the earth. It was simply the Presence of God in their midst."

The son lay his head back, took a slow breath, closed his eyes and mumbled, "The Presence of God in our relationships. Flowing through me and contained in my relationship with my wife."

The father whispered, "Ask Him for help. He will give it to you." As the son slowly drifted off to sleep the father sat and pondered, *The Presence of God was beginning to settle into his relationship with his son.*

1 Matt 18:20
2 John 13:35
3 1Jo 4:12 ,
4 John 17:23
5 Deu. 33

Chapter 5

The next evening the father walked into the room. The son's wife was just leaving. He greeted her and they chatted for a short while. She left and the father settled down next to his son.

"Were you able to talk to her at all?" the father asked.

"A little, probably more than we have in months. She actually asked how I was doing and seemed to care. I think I get the part of my relationship with God and how He wants to flow through me. Can we talk about my relationship with others? Can we begin with my relationship with my wife?"

"That would be the best place to begin. What went wrong?"

"I've given that some thought. I've been too busy and so preoccupied with my desires that I haven't listened to her. I haven't given her any attention. I haven't made any space for her in my life in years."

The father winced, "Ouch, that has hurt her pretty bad. What do you mean there was no space for her in your life?"

"Remember when I was a kid and I begged for a dog as my first pet?"

The father nodded.

"You told me that I would have to make space in my day to take care of it. I would need to play with it, feed it and clean up after it. Do you remember how tired I got of it?"

"I sure do."

"Wait a minute. I think I am seeing something. Let me talk out loud. When I was focused only on me and what I could get from the dog, I got bored. It has been the same for my wife, there was no space for anyone but me. I can't have a relationship without giving that other person space or room in my life, and I can't do that while I am only interested in myself." The son raised his hand to his head, "Oh, I think there's more but I can't quite get it."

"Let me change directions for a moment," the father said, "Let me ask you a question: What is love?"

"I guess for my wife it is giving her some of my space. Recognizing her importance to me and realizing my need for her."

"Where does all love come from?"

"All love must ultimately come from God, for God is love." The son looked at his dad, "True love can only come from God. So He wants His love to flow through me to her. His love is what flows through me. So I can't love her when I am full of myself. That is why I am incomplete alone. I must have someone to express love to in order to be complete in love. So that is why when one of the teachers came and asked Jesus which was the greatest commandment, he said 'Love God with all your heart, soul, mind and strength' and then added the 'Love your neighbor as yourself.' I think I am starting to get it."

"Can I quote some thoughts from God's heart?"

The son nodded and the father continued, "God writes to us and says, 'We know that we have passed from death to life, because we love our brothers. Anyone who does not love remains in death... Dear friends, let us love one another, for love comes from God. Everyone who loves has been born of God and knows God. Whoever does not love does not know God, because God is love...Whoever lives in love lives in God, and God in him.'" [1]

The son's eyes grew teary and he whispered, "I've been dead. I've not loved anyone but myself and that's not love. I understood religion, but never God. I have fooled myself for all these years. No wonder my marriage is a mess. Without God's love it will die as there is no room for true love to flow through me to her."

The father held his son's hand, "You have some thinking and talking to do with God. I think He would like to hear from you."

Tears flowed freely down the son's face. The father sat for a while as the son cried himself to sleep. The father kissed his son's cheek and finally got up to leave.

1 I John 3:14, 3:17, 4:16

Chapter 6

Strength began to build in the son as time slipped by. The father walked in the next day and the son greeted him, "Hey Pop, I'm feeling better and I was looking forward to some more time together. I had a great time with my wife today. We sat and talked for an hour."

"That's great, I am thrilled for the chance for you to start to talk with each other," the father replied, "Let's explore communication and how it helps form a container. How was your dialogue with your wife before the accident?"

"It was almost nonexistent. No, I guess it was just silence followed by loud outbursts and venting followed by more silence. Hmm, does that fit in the category, communication?"

"Yep, it is a form of communication. What did it express?"

"We talked about it yesterday. I had no space in my life for her. I was not interested in anything but me."

"So your communication forms the container, or in your case, it destroys the container."

"What do you mean?"

"I am trying to get you to think. What was going on personally in your heart when the troubles with your relationship began?"

The son lifted the back of his bed higher and settled back into it, "I think I was having trouble at work. I was wondering if I could keep up the pace that my boss expected of me. He hinted I might get fired and that I wasn't fitting in."

"Did you talk with her about it?"

"No, it was work stuff and I didn't want her to worry about it."

"So she didn't know what was going on? Only that you were struggling and having to work much harder?"

The father leaned forward and whispered, "Besides, it was a little hard on your pride to admit it and to think you might not be able to provide for the family."

"I guess so. Okay, I mean, yeah that was a piece of it. Can you imagine how painful it was to talk about?"

The father sat quietly as he let the words settle in. Finally the son said, "So if I can't talk about difficult issues, or painful issues, then I can't build a container?"

"The level of communication will determine the level of relationship you have. The level of relationship will determine how you organize yourselves."

"Whoa," the son called out, "I got the first part but what do you mean by 'it will determine how we organize?'"

"Let me say it another way. In your case, if there is no communication, there is no container. You are just two people bound together by a contract, but not a container."

"I'm beginning to understand but I need more help. We were not a container. That was obvious. We stopped talking and our relationship almost died."

"The issue is trust. If you are talking and hearing each other, then you trust the other person and external structure is not needed. You are not worried about power. If there is no communication, then there is no trust and then you probably told her you were the head of the house and to submit." With the last words the father raised his eyebrows as he looked at his son.

"I do remember using that word a lot recently, as we talked less and less, structure, or maybe I should say me being the boss, became more and more important. So if I am communicating about painful issues then there is a trust established and the structure of our relationship becomes less and less important. Dialogue is what truly holds the container together?"

"You got it. Your ability to communicate will determine the strength of the container you build. You could almost say our words create the container."

"Okay, I have enough to think about," the son declared, "All this talk about pain makes me realize I need some pain killers."

"Take your medicine and we will talk more tomorrow."

Chapter 7

"You seemed to hint that the family is not the only container. You also seemed to imply that communication is the key for all containers," the son began as soon as his Dad walked in the room the next morning.

"You must be getting your strength back. You also must have been woken up a lot last night and had too much time to think."

"That's right. It seemed like hours and hours. Now, what about other containers?"

The father began, "Any time two or three people, or a large group of people join together they form a container. Just as individuals form a container so families form the basis for all other containers. Families form together and make a community. Woven together out of the fabric of relationships established by the families, something beautiful and bigger than the families is created.

"A stained glass window comes to mind. Think of each family as a color or a small leaded area of the window. As they join together they form a larger design that becomes something greater than the individual colors. A picture is born. Or in this case, a larger container is built. A God so awesome and beautiful, so unending in Glory desires many different kinds of containers in order to reveal Himself. He is so good and great that there will never be enough containers to reveal His diverse beauty and greatness."

The son laughed, "I can't help but see this large container, like our community, as one big huge church building. That can't be what you mean."

The father shook his head, "That is a religious view, not God's. Each community is different. It depends on their unique expression and their communication with each other. You might have farming communities, or technology communities, industrial or whatever, the list could go on and on."

"What happens if there is no communication in a larger container?"

"It is the same for any container. If there is no communication then it is just a bunch of people who by chance happen to find themselves in the same place. If they insist for whatever reason, on all staying together then a power structure is needed in order to keep them from hurting each other. There is an interesting story in the Old Testament about the people wanting a structure. I will put it in my own words." [1]

• • •

It was a time of transition for Israel. They were in the midst of becoming a nation and struggling with the process. The leaders came to Samuel and said,

"Samuel, you are an old man and your children cannot give us leadership and wisdom as you have."

"It is painful to agree with you but I know it's true," he replied.

The leaders asked with one voice, "We are tired of having to wrestle with all the problems. We want you to appoint a king over us to lead us so that we can be like the other nations around us."

Samuel just stared in stunned silence. "I don't like that at all. I will seek the Lord for you." With that he left the leaders to seek God.

• • •

"Samuel," God called out.

"Yes, Lord!"

"They don't want me as King."

"I know. May I join you tonight?"

"Yes, I would enjoy your company," the Lord whispered back.

The night was spent together as they wept for the nation of Israel. The morning came slowly and the Lord sent Samuel to warn the people of the folly of their choice. They wanted an earthly king to fill their container.

Samuel walked with his servant on his way to speak to the people. "Samuel, what's wrong with wanting a king? It seems God describes Himself as a King, and He talks about His Kingdom. So what's wrong with the people wanting a king?" his servant asked.

Samuel spoke out his thoughts, "Well, it is a Presence question and in essence a leadership issue. God is the King and has a Kingdom, but the people don't want His Presence and leadership over them. They want to copy the world."

"What's wrong with copying other nations? Can't we learn anything from them?"

Samuel waited for a moment as the donkey brayed, "We can learn many things from other people and nations but this is about who they will serve and listen to. It is about love and authority and where they will find their security."

"So is stability and security wrong?" the servant wondered out loud.

"No, but security and stability will never work if they are our primary desire. If you focus on them as an end then your focus is on the container and not what is in it. A container accommodates, embodies or carry's something. It is a means to an end."

Samuel reached over and pulled out the water skin that was tied to the donkey. He held it up and said, "Let me give you an example. Here is a container. It is a means by which we carry our water. What if I became more concerned with using the skin for something other than carrying the water inside?"

The servant thought for a moment and then said, "It wouldn't be a container anymore, it might become a piece of art or even a weapon. But it would lose the importance of what it does. What it does is carry water."

"That's right. You become more concerned with it, than what it is supposed to do. When that happens you lose the purpose of a container, which is to hold something special. That which is accommodated or contained, loses relevance and becomes secondary."

"So how is that water container like Israel?" the servant inquired.

Samuel stated, "They have forgotten that what makes them special is what they are to hold or carry. They are a chosen people who God has set apart so He can reveal Himself to the world through them. He wants to dwell in their midst, His Presence among them. However, they are more interested in the container, than the beauty of what it holds when God comes down among them. The key question is who will fill the container? They have simply stated, they want a king, not God. They want to be like the world and value a king's glory over God's. They have forgotten that God wants to bless the other nations through them and they want a container that will only bless themselves."

Samuel opened the water skin and began to pour the clear water out. The servant stared as he watched the precious water disappear in the rocky, dry soil. When the water was completely poured out. Samuel threw the water bottle to his servant and said, "It's like you being more interested in the container and not caring about how much water is inside, if it's drinkable or where it comes from."

Samuel took a breath and said, "Now no more questions. I have to pray and think about the people and their desire for a worldly kingdom. They are going to reject my words, but I must be obedient and trust God is bigger than their foolishness."

Samuel stood before the people and began, "This king will use you for his own purposes. He will take the best of your land and give it to his servants, he will take the strongest and most beautiful of your sons and daughters and a tenth of every harvest. At the heart of it, he will make you his servants to accomplish his will."

• • •

The father hesitated and said, "The people's mind had been made up. They refused to listen to Samuel, and therefore, God gave them the presence they wanted."

The son shifted his weight in the bed and the father continued.

• • •

Samuel walked back towards his home with his servant. His head hung low as he thought of the people.

His servant asked, "Master, what's wrong?"

Samuel lifted his head and responded, "My heart aches for the people. They are afraid and won't trust God anymore. They think it will be much easier to trust a king they can see, feel and hear rather than God."

The servant asked, "Is it wrong to want a leader to help them?"

Samuel walked for a while and then responded, "They don't want a leader to help them. They want a leader to control them. They want someone to relieve them of their personal responsibility for building relationships to form a container. It is easier to be told what to do than carry the responsibility they will need to build a national container with God as their leader."

The servant looked over at Samuel and said, "I understand their desire. It's much easier to have you tell me what to do, rather then to take the initiative myself and risk getting to know you well enough to help you make decisions where I know I can. You're old and soon you will be gone and I will be confronted with decisions that I don't want to face. It's much easier to let you make them all and then just to think about serving someone else rather doing what God has for me."

Samuel looked over at his servant, "You understand very well, I just wish the people could see it like you do."

• • •

The son continued to shift his weight, "I'm already tired of this bed." As he settled into a new position he pondered out loud, "They wanted to be like other kingdoms and not let their relationship with God and each other create the structure?"

"That's right," the father affirmed, "When their relationships are shallow they can't deal with the real problems they have with each other and within themselves. Thus the only way they can deal with the problem is through a leader telling them what to do. They want the leader to resolve problems they won't face. Samuel warned them of the problems coming but they wouldn't listen."

"They had the same problem I had. There's no love flowing through them."

"You are a quick learner. They were not interested in love, just power. Which reminds me, I have a meeting I have to go to and try and help resolve a power dispute. I will see you tomorrow."

"Come early and we can watch The Master's tournament. It should be a good day."

"I'll see you then."

1 I Samuel 8

Chapter 8

Hours passed as the father and son watched The Master's golf tournament. Moans and shouts arose as time went by depending on the shots played.

"Okay, I enjoyed that. Now I do have some thoughts. I have been talking with the nurses and doctors and the union is talking about a strike. Is the hospital supposed to be a container? How does their relationship effect the running of a hospital? What about when a strong leader overrules the people?"

"This is the flip side of what we talked about yesterday. You have heard about the Chairman of the Hospital's Board? He's a strong leader that is full of himself. Let me tell you about another leader who was full on himself."1

• • •

Daniel was a righteous man who loved God and was a counselor to the King of one of the strongest nations in his time.

Now, Daniel was in the recent habit of coming to the field and watching the king as he knew the seven year judgment was up. Daniel wanted to see what would happen to this once great king. *What would he learn from this when God gave him back his mind? How would he respond to such humiliation?*

Daniel stood at the edge of the field and looked at the half man, half animal who squatted on his haunches while pulling up handfuls of grass and stuffing it in his mouth. The man's hair was a matted mess and hadn't been cut for seven years. He was completely naked as his clothes had long since worn out and fallen off. His long finger nails were curled over and he had not bathed. Years of grime and filth were caked on him. Grunts emerged from the man as he moved around.

Daniel stood silently and reflected, *Oh King Nebuchadnezzar, look at you as you squat there, you were such a strong and powerful leader over so many. You thought control was yours.*

Images of the king in his glory flooded Daniel's mind.

The conquest over Israel. Riding high on his stallion in full ceremonial gear after returning from the siege. The roar and worship of the crowd and the leaders chained and being dragged behind him. Carts full of gold and precious items. Another victory for the king.

The king strutting about in his beautiful palace and then standing on the edge of the wall and declaring, "Is this not Babylon the great, which I myself have built as a royal residence by the might of my power and for the glory of my majesty?"

Daniel remembered his invitation to work with the king and be a counselor to him. Soon after this invitation, the king had a dream and he required his wise men to tell him what the dream was and what it meant. If they couldn't, they would all die.

Daniel chuckled to himself, *It was impossible to man, but not impossible to God. The King looked so stunned when I told him what it was and what it meant.*

Daniel looked at the man in the field and spoke to him, "You were even willing to acknowledge my God and pay homage to Him. But you promoted me and not His Presence. You quickly forgot Him and were consumed with your own power. You built an image of gold for us to worship and again God revealed his power to you through a fire that could not consume His people. Then you had another dream and He sent me to warn you again of what would happen to you if you would not turn from your arrogance. You simply would not accept that the Most High is ruler over the realm of mankind. He is Lord over all families, communities and nations [containers]."

Daniel unconsciously spoke louder, he was almost yelling, as he understood anew and afresh the foundation that all leaders must learn, "IT IS HEAVEN THAT RULES, GOD IS SOVEREIGN."

He stared in amazement. He knew those were not his words, but God's. As Daniel looked at the filthy, grunting king, it was as if the king understood the words. The once great king, now squatting eating grass, turned and stared at Daniel. Slowly the glazed look in his eyes disappeared and he stood to his feet. He spit out the grass and walked over to Daniel and hugged him and asked through a raspy voice that could barely be understood, "How long have I been like this?"

Daniel, looked into his eyes, "Seven years my king. It is as God spoke to you before. You would be like this for seven years."

The king looked down at himself and the dirt and filth covering him. He reached up and touched his matted hair and beard and then turned to look at the world around him.

He then turned to look to the sky and stated, "Oh Most High, Yours is the only Kingdom that endures, for it is everlasting. All the earth is as nothing compared to You. You are the only true leader and You do according to Your will, in heaven and on earth." He looked at himself, " No one can stop Your power or question You asking, 'What have You done?' You alone have power, and all order is yours. Your Presence is truly the only presence capable of filling any container."

Daniel took off his shawl and placed it around the king while he grabbed Daniel's arm for support and they walked back towards the splendor of his kingdom. As they walked the king declared, "He is able to humble those who think they have control. Such a simple lesson took me so long to learn."

Daniel held his arm and replied, "At least my king, you have learned it. It only took you seven years. Many leaders never do and pay a heavy price."

• • •

The son thought out loud, "So, leaders who are in a position of power think that the container is for them and them alone. They make the container an expression of themselves and put their presence in it. It seems God does not take that lightly."

"That's right. All leaders will be called to account for the influence they have in the container. If they rob God of His Glory filling the container then they will have to answer directly to Him."

"Ooh, I don't think I would want to be the Chairman of the Board. He is only interested in money and power. He's destroying the container."

"A focus on power and the leader's presence filling the container will always cheapen the relationships of those involved and eventually break it up."

The son thought out loud, "I wonder how God's presence would reveal itself in a container known as a hospital?"

"A hospital's purpose is to work with God's created material world and to find and create an ever higher quality of life for all people."

"So that would mean that when money is the priority, the people focus on curing rather than prevention because there is more money in that."

"I hadn't thought of that but you're right and that's one of the reasons why we have so many problems." He stood up to leave, "I have to run. I will see you tomorrow."

1 Daniel 4

Chapter 9

The father appeared the next day and the son was ready to begin. "Dad, I've been thinking some more about containers. I'm glad you finally got here. I've been contemplating how this affects me in my going back to work."

"Well, don't stop now. Keep talking."

"I want to talk about business containers but first I have some quick questions. We talked about different containers last time, what about government? How would God's presence manifest itself there?"

"A government is to provide and ensure justice and equality through the law for the greatest number of citizens."

"Okay, how about education?"

"Education is to provide for the development of the God given gifts in every child for the service of their fellow man and society. But remember the authority for education rests with the parents, not the schools."

"Okay, any more containers?"

"Yeah, for instance, the family is to provide a safe, nurturing environment for growth, values and education of the next generation. Arts and entertainment is to provide rest, relaxation and restoration of the soul through beauty and joy."

"So the different containers express different attributes of God's character and nature? That's why people get so confused when they think all containers have to be religious or like a church!"

"That's right," the father replied, "we think all containers have to be religious but that is not the goal at all. The goal is a relationship with God and others, and then how God wants to reveal His Presence in the container."

"Now, what about business? This is the area I feel I am to work in. How would God's Presence be seen in this container?

"A business container provides needed goods, services and employment opportunities for the community at a fair market price and wage."

"I was thinking of it more as a system of exchange based on fairness. The real challenge nowadays for businesses is creating a flexible container."

"What do you mean?" the father asked.

"Everything is changing and businesses have to constantly change to be competitive."

"This may surprise you but the Bible is the perfect book for that."

"Really, I would never, in a thousand years, have thought that. I figured it was only about getting to heaven and religion."

"It's much, much more. It's about God's desire to create a container that would be flexible enough to fit in any culture and live and grow for thousands of years."

"Tell me a story about the struggles in the New Testament. I want to learn how God was at work and the challenges the people faced."

"The first story has to do with John the Baptist's parents. Zacharias, John's father, was going to have to deal with change and let's see how he responded."

• • •

Zacharias and Elizabeth were righteous and blameless in the sight of God. They were without child and advanced in years. They had offered many prayers to God for a child, with no result. They trusted Him who was Sovereign over all things. His presence dwelling in their relationship was enough.

Zacharias was a priest who was performing his priestly duties. Each section of priests served at the temple for one week, twice a year. It was his time to serve. He was also chosen to enter into the Holy of Holies to burn incense. This privilege came only once in a lifetime. Sometimes, not at all.

He entered the Holy of Holies and soaked in the wonder of being there. Then an angel of the Lord appeared before him. He stared in fear at the shining fire before him and his mind raced ahead, *I am undone. I am a man and I shouldn't be here.*

The angel said, "Don't be afraid, Zacharias, your prayers have been heard and your wife Elizabeth will bear you a son, and you will call him John."

Zacharias listened to the words and tried to slowly take in each one. Questions erupted in his mind, *Elizabeth pregnant? We are both too old. Call him John? No one in my family is named that; what will others say?*

"He will be a great joy to many and great in the sight of God. He will drink no wine and will be filled with the Holy Spirit while in his mother's womb. He will turn back many of the sons of Israel to a relationship with the Lord their God. He will prepare the way of the Lord."

Zacharias' mind raced on, *He will be set aside to God? He will be a forerunner to the Messiah? That will change everything.*

Zacharias finally found words and asked, "How shall I know this for certain?"

The angel answered, "I am Gabriel, and I stand before the presence of God. Your prayer for a child is finally being answered after all these years and you want certainty? OK, you will be mute and not able to speak until the day these things take place. Silence is a wonderful mentor and should give you plenty of time to ponder what part certainty is to play in your life."

Zacharias left the Holy of Holies and wrote out what happened to his fellow priests and quickly went home when his duties were done. He wrote out what happened to explain it to his wife and in time she conceived a child.

Zacharias spent nine months in complete silence pondering his need for certainty and its effect on his family. The morning came when his son was born and he held the wrapped up infant in his arms. His mind wondered over the last months and all he learned:

My little son John. You have taught me so much already and you are only a newborn. I wanted certainty. Your being born was going to bring so much change to us and will bring so much change to Israel that I wanted to be sure. I can see what I really wanted was to be safe. Certainty would keep me safe in all the changes and give me a sense of control. I wanted to trust in myself and my ability to handle change and not God's ability to walk with me through change. I can see how foolish that was. If I am in control and safe, then I don't need faith. I forgot that God is good, sovereign and by faith we overcome. Not by my power and safety.

Zacharias looked up as the people walked in and came to ask Zacharias what the child would be called. He spelled out the name, John.

It was then that his mouth was opened and Zacharias spoke praising God.

• • •

"Why was certainty so wrong?" the son asked.

"Certainty removes faith, he didn't want to have faith and trust God in the midst of the change, he wanted certainty so he could be safe from change," the father stated.

"So any time people put their faith in a culture, family, tradition or even religion, they are looking for certainty in our world, certainty in a container?

"That's right. God says that anything that can be shaken will be shaken. He is the only certainty as He is the only absolute."

"I can see I was looking for certainty in my job, in my position and in my economic status. That's why God let me lose it so I can see how cheap and shallow it was."

"It would seem to be that way. God's love is the only true certainty."

The son thought out loud, "Israel struggled with this for they were not safe in His love. They couldn't accept the changes God wanted to bring."

The father smiled and asked, "Have you ever carefully wrapped a gift and then looked in anticipation to the time when the person will open it up?"

"Sure, I can think of a time a few years ago when I bought presents for my wife."

"Then you can understand how God felt as he did this for mankind. The Hebrews were the container He would place the gift in before He wrapped it. He spent two thousand years in preparing them for the right moment. Making sure each element of the package was just right so when the gift was placed inside it would fit perfectly.

"With anticipation God looked forward to the day when he could come through the container that was so carefully prepared and enter our world to bring good news. A blessing given to all the nations."

"I guess I know, but I will ask anyway. How did the Hebrew people respond?" The father bowed and said, "Thank you for asking. They became so enthralled with the box that they forgot all about the present it was holding. They clung to the box as if it was the most important part. Like a beautifully wrapped box, they became so enthralled with themselves, their culture and their religion that they forgot what they were there for."

"I get it. They placed their security in themselves and forgot about God and how he wanted to reveal himself. Silly people."

"Before you pick up a stone to throw at them, think about how every successful business has become distracted with themselves and are often unable to change. Their own success breeds failure, because they trust in the way things were done in the past.

"In fact every major revival has eventually had this happen to it. A group of people meet together to seek God's Presence and pray. He shows up and reveals His Presence and it isn't too many years before there is a denominational container built around it. Let more years slip by and The Presence of God isn't the important part anymore. It is how things are done that becomes the priority. The container has more priority than The Presence.

"Israel would rather kill Jesus than change. That is a lesson I should remember," the son pondered out loud.

Chapter 10

"Tell me more dad. What were the struggles Jesus faced?" the son asked.

"Okay, let me put them in story form and see what we can learn."

• • •

"Jesus," the disciples of John the Baptist called out.

"Yes," he replied.

"Why are the religious leaders and ourselves fasting and you and your disciples are feasting? Have you no respect for the container God has shown us to make, so that His Presence may dwell among us?"

"It is a time of celebration, for God is doing a new thing. Fasting will be appropriate later," Jesus replied.

• • •

The father added, "To help them understand the deeper issues of their question, Jesus gave them a parable about containers."

• • •

"You don't put a new patch on old clothes do you? Nor do you put new wine in old skins? You must use a new container when you are dealing with new things," Jesus added.

As was his custom, Jesus later pulled his disciples aside and discussed everything with them.

One of them asked him, "Jesus, why did you answer their question about fasting and religious works with examples of clothes and wineskins?"

"Their focus is on the container and not what it was to hold."

Jesus hesitated and looked at their face and when he saw their lack of understanding he continued on, "Clothes are a way of serving the body of the one who wears them. A wineskin is there to accommodate the new wine. If the clothes or wineskin will not cover the body or hold the wine then they must be replaced. Imagine a man who would still try and fit into children's clothes. In times past, God gave the Israelites revelation of who He was that is held in a Jewish container. The Jews were the people that God choose to reveal himself to and they held a revelation of who He was through their relationship with Him and their relationships with each other.

"However, you cannot form a container based on what was appropriate in the past and then demand that God come and fill it because He has done it before. That is more like magic than how God works. When God is doing a new thing, patching old traditions or just adding new pieces to it will not work."

"How then can any of our people's traditions be trusted?" one disciple asked in astonishment.

"Traditions cannot be trusted by themselves, but only in that they reveal The Presence of Him who formed them. There is much to learn from the traditions of those who have gone before us. The life is not in the traditions, but in The Presence of God revealed through them. You must cling to who God was in the container, not the container itself. Who He revealed Himself to be in The Law and through the prophets will be the same God revealed here, only greater. Unless you are willing to lay aside the old container and look to God for a new one, you will miss the point of a container. His name, His identity, His Presence is the only thing we can cling to, nothing else will last."

Jesus continued on, "The revelation that God gave to them was to prepare them for this day. All that God has done in the past was to point to how He would reveal himself today. But they have become distracted with the past rather than what the past held and pointed to."

"What did the past hold and what was it pointing too?" one of the disciples blurted out.

"The past held God and was the preparation for me in all He did. I AM the fulfillment of all that has gone before me."

The disciples just sat there and stared, trying to comprehend the words just spoken.

Jesus continued on, "They are trying to cling to the container and have forgotten what it was to hold. I AM that which must fill all containers or the containers will crumble."

• • •

"He understood the challenges we face today. Two thousand years ago they wrestled with the same issues we wrestle with today," the son stammered out loud, "They were stuck just like we get stuck."

"Some things never change. In fact if you had listened in on the Pharisees they might have sounded something like this:

• • •

"We are God's chosen people. That's what we need to remember. That's all that matters," the leader declared and then listened to others state their case.

"But this Jesus is capturing the attention of all the people. He is even working miracles. They say he raised Lazarus from the dead. His Presence has power to do things never seen before."

An arrogant one quickly replied, "Yes, but he is not keeping all our traditions. We have had these traditions and laws since our father Moses. Moses gave us clear guidelines that we have interpreted clearly and this Jesus is not obeying them. They are the only expression of God's Presence. They define who we are and how we are to relate."

"Yes, God has shown us we are special and therefore we must protect ourselves."

A loud one in the back declared, "If the voice of our fathers is not clear, our people will lose their place in the world. What God has given to our fathers is the only thing that matters."

"He is breaking the Sabbath. We must stop him."

The leader interrupted, "God has told us that He does not change. Therefore what we know about Him from the past will not change. We know the truth and it is that the Sabbath is Holy and that is all we need to know."

The heat of the conversation grew as still more voices joined in.

"The only thing we can trust is our traditions and laws that define who we are. They give the people a stable and safe place to live. It is our people's presence in this terrible place we must watch out for."

A fearful one reminded them, "Rome would love to remove our presence from here. We must protect what He has given to us in order to keep Him dwelling among us."

An angry one spit out, "We must cut off anyone or anything that will try and take what God has given to us. It must be protected at all costs."

"This Jesus is not one of us. He has not submitted to us. He talks with the Gentiles. He mingles with prostitutes. He eats with sinners. He is even said to be conceived out of wedlock. He acts as if we are not a special people and wants to put us on the same level as the sinners around us. If he were from God he would never stoop to touch those heathen."

The leader arose and raised his hand, "Then it is agreed. We must lead and make the decision that is best for the people. Jesus must be stopped. He must die."

A chorus arose around the leader with one voice, "Yes."

• • •

"If you changed some of the words they might have sounded like some of the people in the office at work. You hear things like: 'This is the way we do things.' 'Don't rock the boat.' 'The policies state that...'"

"Fuel for more thought," the father stated as he got up. "I have some errands to run and I will see you tomorrow. Sleep good," the father said as he walked out the door.

"Sleep good, " the son mumbled, "That's a good joke in a hospital."

Chapter 11

The son wondered out loud as he sat with his father, "We all have a need to fit into a container, to be a member, included and a part of something bigger than ourselves. I wanted to fit in with the guys in my office. Why was that? What happened?"

"Even though people are not interested in walking in a relationship with God and letting His love flow through them it doesn't mean they don't desire to be a part of a container. The healthy desire, given by God, gets distorted and bent and causes all kinds of problems. You can no more remove a natural desire that God put within you than you can remove the desire to see with your eyes, hear with your ears or speak with your tongue."

"Tell me more. This is significant for me but I don't see it clear enough yet. How does it cause problems?"

The father smiled, "Remember when you stole the chewing tobacco, even though you didn't chew, just so you would fit in? You were caught and paid a heavy price for that."

The son shook his head, "I remember."

"What about the clothes you used to wear just so you could hang out and be a part of the right group?"

"Do you remember how painful it was when you got cut from the team and you felt so bad you vowed it would never happen again?" All that hard work to be a jock and 'fit in' with the 'real men' in school?"

The son thought back and stated, "I can see it in every stage of my life. I wanted to be accepted by those that were cool. I wanted to be a part of the 'in' group."

The father asked, "Why do you think gangs have such an appeal to kids this days? Their families are not containers anymore, they seek to be a part of the gang who takes the place of their family. A desire to belong to a container is one of the great, permanent emotional wellsprings of humanity. Through God, love is the only way we can do it. Without Him we struggle trying to fit into the world's system of containers.

Let me give you an illustration from a game we play that might help. Life becomes like a game of musical chairs. The music begins and people start to move around, anxious, looking for their place. There are purposively not enough chairs for everyone. Some one must be left standing on the outside or there is no use playing. Those left standing are cut off from the in-group. They are not as important as those still in the game. Those sitting are among the in-group, thankfully still a part of the game. The feeling of having made it lasts only for a moment."

The father stopped while the son shifted his weight and then continued, "The game continues and there is more starting and stopping of music, more wrestling and less smiles. The crowd watching becomes larger and those still in the game are more aware of their status. As you are sitting there, you are linked with a few others that are admired, accepted, a part of a group, validated. You are on the inside. What makes this feeling so wonderful? For a brief moment you're a part of a container. There are outsiders looking in and you know you are where they want to be.

"In the end it is only two people with one chair. The music begins and when it stops there is a struggle and one person is sitting down and the other is left standing. The person standing up is out of the game. The person sitting is the winner. Or is he? As a result of winning the game, he or she is alone. There is no one left to relate to. The game quickly starts over."

Tears formed in the son's eyes as he listened.

"The world's containers are built around competition and there is never enough room. To find acceptance, you have to stay in the group. You have to find and keep your place. Yet soon the music starts, the competition begins and you are up and moving around with another chair gone. You are confronted with the possibility that this time you may be left out if you don't try harder. Forever pushing and shoving to stay in the game only to find out when the game is over that victory leaves you all alone. If you want open and deep relationships, and that is what we were made for, there's no way to win the game. There is no winner."

Tears flowed freely as the son saw his own struggle, "That's me. I have longed to be a part of a team my whole life. I thought I would find it with my wife but that wasn't working. I thought I could find it at my job, but that wasn't working. I could never find it in the world's containers. How do I deal with this desire dad?"

"Take the desire to fit in to the Cross and lay it there and declare before Him that He will be the source of your acceptance. He and He alone is the only One who can truly give life. Through His love is the only way that true, eternal, unconditional relationships take place. If you give up your desire to fit-in, if you die to a place in the world, then a surprising result will follow. You will be free from its hold on your life and you will find your place in God where he will join you together with others as a natural expression for His Presence. When you die to the desire to fit in, you will find for the first time in your life you have the beginning of a container that God can dwell in.

"Let me tell you a paraphrase of the way I think Jesus might have said it."

• • •

Jesus reached into a bowl that was full of grapes and raised up a handful of them and stated, "I am the true vine. My father is the vine dresser. Every branch that does not bear fruit from its relation-ship with me, my Father will take it away. The branches that bear fruit, He prunes that you bear more fruit. Abide in me and you will bear much fruit. Apart from me you can do nothing."

He continued, "I am leaving soon and you must follow later. I have work for you to do."

Jesus pulled a towel from the table and laid it out, "Fruit is not to be left on the vine where it will fall to the ground and rot. It is to be picked and prepared. Given as a drink to the thirsty."

Jesus filled the towel with grapes and then rolled the towel around the grapes. He handed one end of the towel to one of the disciples and while handing the other end to another he said, "Twist the towel."

As they began to twist the towel, Jesus reached out and grabbed it in the middle and began to crush the grapes. A slow trickle of juice began to drop from the towel. One of the disciples quickly grabbed the bowl and set it under the dripping towel. They all watched as juice poured forth into the bowl slowly filling it.

"If you abide in me, then you will produce fruit. This fruit must be prepared and put into a container. Allow yourselves to be broken and crushed. As a grape must be crushed to produce wine, so you must be crushed to release The Presence of God in your midst."

"You ask, what is the container Lord that will hold Your presence?"

"Just as I am in the Father and the Father is in me, so I now say to you, Just as we are one, so you are to be one. Your relationships with each other will form the container that will hold our presence in your midst. By this shall all men know you are my disciples. If you have love one for another."

• • •

The son lay there and wept as revelation washed over him. He mumbled, "I don't have to fit in to be accepted. I don't have to struggle to find my place."

The father stood up and kissed his son on the forehead and said, "I can see you have some more reflection and talking to do with God. I will see you tomorrow."

Chapter 12

The father walked into the room just as his wife was leaving. She gave the father a big hug and whispered in his ear, "Thank you for all you're doing. I want to talk with you later. However, right now I have a meeting I must run to."

The father whispered back, "I would love to spend more time with you. I look forward to it."

The son's wife left the room and the father walked over and sat next to his son. Tears were streaming down his son's eyes. The father prodded, "You haven't been crying all night have you?"

"No, we just had one of the richest, most open conversations we have ever had. I shared my heart and she shared her heart. I think for the first time in a while we feel like something is happening in our relationship. There is hope. Thanks Dad."

"You're welcome."

The son continued, "I have learned more in the last couple of weeks than I have in my whole lifetime. I think I may finally be ready to grow up. I was wondering, did the struggle to find a container for God's people end with Jesus' death and resurrection?" the son asked.

"No," the father replied, "look at the church in Corinth and listen to their struggle."

• • •

The argument began again, "I was baptized by Paul!"

Another voice arose, "I was taught by Apollos!"

"But Paul himself saw Jesus, He had a

revelation of Heaven. He is our founder."

"Yes but he left us and Apollos came and taught us. He was with us and explained what it all meant. That makes him our leader."

"We must decide who we are with. They are different leaders and we must decide who has authority here."

"All I know is that Paul baptized me. He is the only one I will listen too."

•   •   •

"What do you think they were struggling with?" the father asked.

"It sounds like whose presence was in the container. Who they would identify with and follow?"

"That's right. After Jesus was gone, the struggle continued. Paul wrote a letter to the church and in a paraphrase, it sounded something like this:

• • •

Word has reached me that you are not acting like spiritual men. You are mere children, babies in Christ. Why do I say this?

There is jealousy and strife among you as you try and argue and live as the world does.

Some of you argue that you are with me. Others have taken Apollo's side. What is this argument? We are mere individuals, servants of God doing what God has given us a heart to do.

I have a gift to bring, Apollos has a gift to bring. Are you trying to build a container around our gifts and identity? Don't be so foolish and worldly minded. We are only pieces of the container. If we neglect part of a container to emphasize another we all lose out. It is only Jesus who can be the true identity and it is His Presence that can bring life. Nothing or no one else can fill that role. Each person in the group has something to give and must relate with each other. As this happens God will Presence Himself among you.

God, who knows the hearts of each man, will reward each one for the work they are involved in. Do not put us in God's role. He alone can bring life. He alone will judge the work each one plays in using his gifts and developing relationships among the people. My brethren build a container that God may fill with His Presence.

• • •

"Why all the struggle dad? This may sound crazy, but why not just patiently wait for God to return and take us out of this mess?"

"Because the most powerful message we have is found in the container we build. What was that movie, 'if we build it, they will come.' God deeply loves everyone in this world. If we will build a container for Him to dwell in, the world will listen to us. If we can't build a container for His Presence then we have proven we do not have love flowing through us and we have no message to offer the world. Who we are is speaking so loud they can't hear what we are saying."

"I think I understand," the son replied, "It is all about relationships."

After a silence seemed to warmly wrap around them the son finally broke it, "I feel like this is the best thing that ever happened to me. I only hope we can build on it and get back what I have thrown away."

"We have made a good start at that. I look forward to more time together, even when you are not a captive audience."

"I will be glad to get our of here, that's for sure."

Epilogue

Hold on to your faith friends, if you think God has moved in the past, you haven't seen anything yet. I believe He has one more container to raise us to, beyond anything we have yet seen.

Just as He began a new container for the early church with sound of wind and tongues of fire, so the last days shall be filled with revealing a new work of His Presence and power.

Just as God planned thousands of years to prepare the Jews for a new container that He would release through them, so now, God has planned thousands of years for a new container to be released through us. We have known a cleansing and purging of our leaders and churches. We have been and are being tested in every way possible. This new container will be the final container in that it will be the last and the greatest container that will hold the presence of God for the final revival, reformation and restoration of God dwelling within us.

With this remarkable indwelling, The Body of Christ as a container will finally come of age. A container, within containers, within containers, within containers, people from every nation, tribe, people and tongue, orchestrating themselves and responding in faith, pure, transparent and alive in relationships, as God gives the fullest expression of Himself that the world has ever known.

About the Author

Matt Rawlins was born on the West Coast and grew up in a Christian home. He jokes that his earliest prayer was "Lord, help me not to swear." It seemed clear to him that if you didn't swear, you were a good person and if you were a good person, you could avoid hell and go to heaven. After all, wasn't that the purpose of heaven? To avoid hell?

In his late teens God began to stir his mind and he remembers sitting with his family around a dinner table and asking, "What is love?" It seems that question led him in desperation to find out if there was a real source of love or if the world was just a bad dream.

It was through this searching that Matt ended up doing a training program with Youth With A Mission (YWAM). He recalls, "One time when I was crying before God, words came to me that seemed to sum up my whole life. The words were 'I'm so lonely, I'm so lonely.' It was then that I realized Christianity was a relationship of love and not fear. I guess it was then that I realized how much Jesus loved me and I fell in love with him."

He volunteered with YWAM and spent three years working in Saipan, Micronesia. From there, he went on to Hong Kong where he met his beautiful wife, Celia, (she is from Hawaii) and they were married. After a year in Hong Kong they moved to Singapore to take over the YWAM work there. Their son, Joshua was born there. They were in Singapore for five years.

Later they moved to Oregon where Matt's family was living, and Matt went back to school. He finished his BA in Management and Communications; currently Matt, 41, is working to finish his doctorate in leadership development and communication.

Currently the Rawlins family lives in Kailua - Kona, Hawaii and Matt is finishing his dissertation. He also works with YWAM and is involved in training and teaching all over the world in leadership development.

Interested in More?

A*muze*ment Publications

produces a series of books that captures the hearts of readers and provokes them to '*muze*' over who God is, who they are and the part they are to play in the world around them.

The Question

Is God good to all?
Who God is and how we view Him is
The Question we are all confronted
with. The story moves through creation
and explores the devil's attack against
God's character. It focuses on Job's
struggle with The Question and finishes
with how God answered The Question
through Jesus and in His coming final
judgment.

The Namer

God created us in His image. A primary
part of that is our ability to give mean-
ing to the world around us by naming it.
The only limitation God placed on us
was that we could not name ourselves.
When we took that on through our
rebellion against Him, we can see the
troubles and difficulties it caused in our
world. The story follows Saul and David
and looks at how they named themselves and the challenges they faced
because of that.

Emails from Hell
Executive emails from below. How to bring down a leader and an organization. This book is a take off on C. S. Lewis' work. Explore the bent wisdom of a senior demon as he tries to train a young demon in the art of using his subject (a leader) and his organization to accomplish their own purposes.

Books Pending

The Gate and other short stories
A collection of short stories that deals with working together in unity called 'The Dance,' hardship called 'The Craftsman,' giving our gifts to God called 'The Song,' dealing with bitterness called 'Raising a Grudge,' and many, many more.
Christian.

The Conversation
God created us to have an intimate relationship with Him. An important part of any relationship is the ability to communicate with each other. In Christianity we call a part of this conversa-

tion, prayer. What are the ingredients in a good conversation with God? How can we learn to pray and touch His heart? This story looks at the life of prayer in our relationship with God.

The View
What would different people who had been touched by Jesus in His ministry see when they stood and watched Jesus die? How would seeing Him in power and then at His crucifixion affect their view of God? "The View" explores different people's view of Jesus on the cross and how it affected them.

The Line
What part does the law play in our lives as Christians? In this story the law is described as a line that God has drawn for us not to cross. What happened when we did and how are we to deal with lines drawn by men? This story explores what part lines play as boundaries in our lives and how we are to live in freedom within the context of the lines God has drawn for us.

The Classroom
What if our world were a classroom and God was the master teacher? This story explores how God works to teach us principles and values about His kingdom and how we as His students can learn to have a fuller life with our teacher's help.

The Choice
What part does our choice make in our Christian life and how is it an expression of humility? This story explores the life of Moses and how through the different choices he made, God called him the humblest man on the face of the earth.

Any of the books in print can be ordered through any bookstore.

Contact us at:

Our Web Site: **amuzement.com**

Email: info@amuzement.com

Address:
A*muze*ment Publications
7085 Battlecreek Rd. S.E.
Salem, Oregon 97301

Any of the books published by Amuzement
may be ordered through your local book-
stores or at Amazon.com.

9 781928 715054